Preparing for Marriage

SERVICES FROM THE BOOK OF COMMON PRAYER 2004
AND READINGS RECOMMENDED FOR THE MARRIAGE SERVICE

First published in 2004 by
the columba press
55A Spruce Avenue, Stillorgan Industrial Park, Blackrock, Co Dublin

Designed by Bill Bolger
Origination in FF Scala by The Columba Press
Printed in Ireland by Paceprint Ltd, Dublin

ISBN 1 85607 450 1

Table of Contents

Introduction

This booklet provides the services for Marriage in the Church of Ireland authorised by the General Synod and included in the *Book of Common Prayer* for use on and from 6th June 2004. Services are included both in traditional and contemporary language together with a *Form of Prayer and Dedication after a Civil Marriage.* The recommended scripture readings listed in the *Marriage Two* service are printed in full from the *New Revised Standard Version.*

The use of this booklet is recommended for preparation purposes so that an inexpensive and accessible resource may be given to couples as they prepare for their wedding in the Church of Ireland.

Marriage Services

THE FORM OF
SOLEMNIZATION OF MATRIMONY

Introduction

The priest says to the congregation

Dearly beloved, we are gathered together here in the sight of God, and in the face of this congregation, to join together this man and this woman in holy matrimony; which is an honourable estate, instituted of God in the time of man's innocency, signifying unto us the mystical union that is betwixt Christ and his Church; which holy estate Christ adorned and beautified with his presence, and first miracle that he wrought, in Cana of Galilee; and is commended in Holy Scripture to be honourable among all men: and therefore is not by any to be enterprised, nor taken in hand, unadvisedly, lightly, or wantonly; but reverently, discreetly, advisedly, soberly, and in the fear of God; duly considering the causes for which matrimony was ordained:

First, for the increase of mankind, according to the will of God, and for the due ordering of families and households, that children might be brought up in the fear and nurture of the Lord, and to the praise of his holy Name;

Secondly, for the hallowing of the union betwixt man and woman, and for the avoidance of sin;

Thirdly, for the mutual society, help, and comfort, that the one ought to have of the other, both in prosperity and adversity.

Into which holy estate these two persons present come now to be joined. Therefore if any man can shew any just cause why they may not lawfully be joined together, let him now speak, or else hereafter for ever hold his peace.

The minister says to the couple

I require and charge you both, as ye will answer at the dreadful day of judgment when the secrets of all hearts shall be disclosed, that if either of you know any impediment, why ye may not be lawfully joined together in matrimony, ye do now confess it. For be ye well assured, that so many as are coupled together otherwise than God's Word doth allow are not joined together by God; neither is their matrimony lawful.

The Marriage

The minister says to the man

.... Wilt thou have this woman to thy wedded wife, to live together after God's ordinance in the holy estate of matrimony? Wilt thou love her, comfort her, honour, and keep her, in sickness and in health; and, forsaking all other, keep thee only unto her, so long as ye both shall live?
I will.

The minister says to the woman

.... Wilt thou have this man to thy wedded husband, to live together after God's ordinance in the holy estate of matrimony? Wilt thou love him, honour, and keep him, in sickness and in health; and forsaking all other, keep thee only unto him, so long as ye both shall live?
I will.

Or the minister may say to the woman

.... Wilt thou have this man to thy wedded husband, to live together after God's ordinance in the holy estate of matrimony? Wilt thou obey him and serve him, love, honour, and keep him, in sickness and in health; and forsaking all other, keep thee only unto him, so long as ye both shall live?
I will.

The minister asks

Who giveth this woman to be married to this man?

The minister receives the woman at her father's or friend's hands.

THE MARRIAGE VOWS

The man, with his right hand taking the woman by her right hand, says after the minister

I .... take thee .... to my wedded wife, to have and to hold from this day forward, for better for worse, for richer for poorer, in sickness and in health, to love and to cherish, till death us do part, according to God's holy ordinance; and thereto I plight thee my troth.

The woman, with her right hand taking the man by his right hand, says after the minister

I .... take thee .... to my wedded husband, to have and to hold from this day forward, for better for worse, for richer for poorer, in sickness and in health, to love and to cherish, till death us do part, according to God's holy ordinance; and thereto I give thee my troth.

Or the woman, with her right hand taking the man by his right hand, says after the minister

I .... take thee .... to my wedded husband, to have and to hold from this day forward, for better for worse, for richer for poorer, in sickness and in health, to love, cherish, and to obey, till death us do part, according to God's holy ordinance; and thereto I give thee my troth.

GIVING AND RECEIVING OF A RING

The man gives to the woman a ring, laying it on the book.

The man puts the ring on the fourth finger of the woman's left hand and, holding the ring there, says

With this ring I thee wed, with my body I thee worship, and with all my worldly goods I thee endow: In the Name of the Father, and of the Son, and of the Holy Spirit. Amen.

If the woman gives the man a ring, she puts the ring on the fourth finger of the man's left hand and, holding the ring there, says

With this ring I thee wed, with my body I thee worship, and with all my worldly goods I thee endow: In the Name of the Father, and of the Son, and of the Holy Spirit. Amen.

PRAYER

The man and the woman kneel. The priest says

Let us pray.

O eternal God, Creator and Preserver of all mankind, Giver of all spiritual grace, the Author of everlasting life; Send thy blessing upon these thy servants, this man and this woman, whom we bless in thy Name; that, as Isaac and Rebecca lived faithfully together, so these persons may surely perform and keep the vow and covenant betwixt them made (whereof this ring given and received is a token and pledge), and may ever remain in perfect love and peace together, and live according to thy laws; through Jesus Christ our Lord. **Amen.**

Joining their right hands together, the priest says
Those whom God hath joined together let no man put asunder.

The minister speaks to the people
Forasmuch as .... and .... have consented together in holy wedlock, and have witnessed the same before God and this company, and thereto have given and pledged their troth either to other, and have declared the same by giving and receiving of a ring, and by joining of hands; I pronounce that they be man and wife together: In the Name of the Father, and of the Son, and of the Holy Spirit. **Amen.**

The minister adds this Blessing:
God the Father, God the Son, God the Holy Spirit, bless, preserve, and keep you; the Lord mercifully with his favour look upon you; and so fill you with all spiritual benediction and grace, that ye may so live together in this life, that in the world to come ye may have life everlasting. **Amen.**

The minister goes to the Lord's Table.
One of the following Psalms (or a Psalm from the list on page 18) is said or sung.

Psalm 128 **Beati omnes**
1   Blessed are all they that fear the Lord, ▪
    and walk in his ways.
2   For thou shalt eat the labours of thine hands; ▪
    O well is thee, and happy shalt thou be.
3   Thy wife shall be as the fruitful vine ▪
    upon the walls of thine house.
4   Thy children like the olive-branches ▪
    round about thy table.

5   Lo, thus shall the man be blessed ■
     that feareth the Lord.

6   The Lord from out of Sion shall so bless thee ■
     that thou shalt see Jerusalem in prosperity all thy life long.

7   Yea, that thou shalt see thy children's children ■
     and peace upon Israel.

       Glory be to the Father, ■
       and to the Son, and to the Holy Spirit;
       as it was in the beginning, ■
       is now, and ever shall be, world without end. Amen.

or Psalm 67 Deus misereatur

1   God be merciful unto us, and bless us; ■
     and shew us the light of his countenance,
       and be merciful unto us:

2   That thy way may be known upon earth, ■
     thy saving health among all nations.

3   Let the people praise thee, O God; ■
     yea, let all the people praise thee.

4   O let the nations rejoice and be glad, ■
     for thou shalt judge the folk righteously,
       and govern the nations upon earth.

5   Let the people praise thee, O God; ■
     yea, let all the people praise thee.

6   Then shall the earth bring forth her increase, ■
     and God, even our own God, shall give us his blessing.

7   God shall bless us, ■
     and all the ends of the world shall fear him.

       Glory be to the Father, ■
       and to the Son, and to the Holy Spirit;
       as it was in the beginning, ■
       is now, and ever shall be, world without end. Amen.

The man and the woman kneel before the Lord's Table, the minister says
Let us pray.

Lord, have mercy upon us.
Christ, have mercy upon us.
Lord, have mercy upon us.

Our Father, who art in heaven,
hallowed be thy Name,
thy kingdom come,
thy will be done,
On earth as it is in heaven.
Give us this day our daily bread.
And forgive us our trespasses
as we forgive those who trespass against us.
And lead us not into temptation,
but deliver us from evil. Amen.

O Lord, save thy servant, and thy handmaid,
who put their trust in thee.

O Lord, send them help from thy holy place;
and evermore defend them.

Be unto them a tower of strength;
from the face of their enemy.

O Lord, hear our prayer;
and let our cry come unto thee.

O God of Abraham, God of Isaac, God of Jacob, bless these thy servants, and sow the seed of eternal life in their hearts; that whatsoever in thy holy Word they shall profitably learn, they may in deed fulfil the same. Look, O Lord, mercifully upon them from heaven, and bless them. And as thou didst send thy blessing upon Abraham and Sarah, to their great comfort, so vouchsafe to send thy blessing upon these thy servants; that they obeying thy will, and alway being in safety under thy protection, may abide in thy love unto their lives' end; through Jesus Christ our Lord. **Amen.**

This prayer may follow:

O merciful Lord and heavenly Father, by whose gracious blessing mankind is increased; Bestow, we beseech thee, on these thy servants the heritage and gift of children, and grant that they may also live together so long in godly love and honesty, that they may see their children christianly and virtuously brought up, to thy praise and honour; through Jesus Christ our Lord. **Amen.**

O God, who by thy mighty power hast made all things of nothing; who also (after other things set in order) didst appoint, that out of man (created after thine own image and similitude) woman should take her beginning; and, knitting them together, didst teach that it should never be lawful to put asunder those whom thou by Matrimony hadst made one: O God, who hast so consecrated the state of Matrimony, that in it is signified and represented the spiritual marriage and unity betwixt Christ and his Church: Look mercifully upon these thy servants, that both this man may love his wife, according to thy Word (as Christ did love his spouse the Church, who gave himself for it, loving and cherishing it even as his own flesh), and also that this woman may be loving and amiable, faithful and obedient to her husband; and in all quietness, sobriety, and peace, be a follower of holy and godly matrons. O Lord, bless them both, and grant them to inherit thy everlasting kingdom; through Jesus Christ our Lord. **Amen.**

Prayers from those on pages 24-27 may be preferred.

Almighty God, who at the beginning did create our first parents, Adam and Eve, and did sanctify and join them together in marriage; Pour upon you the riches of his grace, sanctify and bless you, that ye may please him both in body and soul, and live together in holy love unto your lives' end. **Amen.**

Unless there is to be a celebration of the Holy Communion a reading from Holy Scripture follows. If there is a sermon it is preached here.

Here may follow an anthem or hymn.

If there is no Communion, the minister says

Let us pray.

O eternal God, we humbly beseech thee favourably to behold these thy servants .... and .... now joined in wedlock according to thy holy ordinance; and grant that they, seeking first thy kingdom and righteousness, may obtain the manifold blessings of thy grace; through Jesus Christ our Lord. **Amen.**

O almighty Lord, and everlasting God, vouchsafe, we beseech thee, to direct, sanctify, and govern both our hearts and bodies, in the ways of thy laws, and in the works of thy commandments; that through thy most mighty protection, both here and ever, we may be preserved in body and soul; through our Lord and Saviour Jesus Christ. **Amen.**

The grace of our Lord Jesus Christ, and the love of God, and the fellowship of the Holy Spirit be with us all evermore. **Amen.**

It is appropriate that the newly married couple should receive the Holy Communion at the time of their Marriage, or at the first opportunity after their Marriage.

THE COLLECT

O eternal God, we humbly beseech thee favourably to behold these thy servants now joined in wedlock according to thy holy ordinance; and grant that they, seeking first thy kingdom and righteousness, may obtain the manifold blessings of thy grace; through Jesus Christ our Lord. **Amen.**

THE EPISTLE

Ephesians 5: 20-33

Giving thanks always for all things unto God and the Father, in the Name of our Lord Jesus Christ; submitting yourselves one to another in the fear of God. Wives, submit yourselves unto your own husbands, as unto the Lord. For the husband is the head of the wife, even as Christ is the head of the church: and he is the saviour of the body. Therefore as the church is subject unto Christ; so let the wives be to their own husbands in every thing. Husbands, love your wives, even as Christ also loved the church, and gave himself for it; that he might sanctify and cleanse it with the washing of water by the Word, that he might present it to himself a glorious church, not having spot, or wrinkle, or any such thing; but that it should be holy and without blemish. So ought men to love their wives as their own bodies. He that loveth his wife loveth himself: for no man ever yet hated his own flesh; but nourisheth and cherisheth it, even as the Lord the church: for we are members of his body, of his flesh, and of his bones. For this cause shall a man leave his father and mother, and shall be joined unto his wife; and they two shall be one flesh. This is a great mystery: but I speak concerning Christ and the church. Nevertheless let every one of you in particular so love his wife even as himself; and the wife see that she reverence her husband.

THE GOSPEL

Matthew 19: 4-6

Jesus said, Have ye not read, that he which made them at the beginning made them male and female, and said, For this cause shall a man leave father and mother, and shall cleave to his wife; and they twain shall be one flesh? Wherefore they are no more twain, but one flesh. What therefore God hath joined together, let not man put asunder.

Or readings from the list on page 18 may be preferred.

On the day of the marriage if anyone alleges or declares any impediment why the man and woman may not lawfully marry, the person alleging or declaring the impediment is required to deposit, or by sureties guarantee, such sum as would cover the cost of the wedding and of all other expenses incurred in connection therewith. The wedding must then be deferred until such time as the truth is tried. Should the impediment not be upheld the amount deposited or guaranteed shall become the property of the man and woman, and the person alleging or declaring the impediment shall be liable for the legal costs incurred.

THE MARRIAGE SERVICE

The Entry

The people stand.

The minister may greet the bridal or marriage party with:
Blessed are they who come in the name of the Lord.
We bless you from the house of the Lord.
O give thanks to the Lord, for he is good,
For his steadfast love endures for ever. *Psalm 118: 26; 136: 1 (adapted)*

A hymn may be sung or instrumental music played during the entrance.

GREETING

The Lord be with you
and also with you.

The minister may say
God is love, and those who live in love live in God,
and God lives in them.   *1 John 4: 16*

The Introduction

The minister says
We have come together in the presence of God
to witness the marriage of .... and ....,
to ask his blessing on them
and to share in their joy.
Our Lord Jesus Christ was himself a guest
at a wedding at Cana of Galilee,
and through his Spirit he is with us now.
The scriptures set before us marriage as part of God's creation
and a holy mystery
in which man and woman become one flesh.

It is God's purpose that, as husband and wife
give themselves to each other
in love throughout their lives,
they shall be united in that love
as Christ is united with his Church.

Marriage was ordained that husband and wife
may comfort and help each other,
living faithfully together in plenty and in need,
in sorrow and in joy.

It is intended that with delight and tenderness
they may know each other in love,
and through the joy of their bodily union
they may strengthen the union of their hearts and lives.

It is intended that they may be blessed
in the children they may have,
in caring for them and in bringing them up
in accordance with God's will
to his praise and glory.

In marriage husband and wife begin a new life together in the community.
It is a permanent commitment that all should honour.
It must not be undertaken carelessly, lightly or selfishly,
but by God's help, with reverence, responsibility,
respect and the promise to be faithful.

This is a way of life, created and hallowed by God,
that .... and .... are now about to begin.
They will each give their consent to the other;
they will join hands and exchange solemn vows,
and in token of this they will give and receive a ring.

Therefore on this their wedding day we pray with them,
that, strengthened and guided by God,
they may fulfil his purpose
for the whole of their earthly life together.

The minister says
Almighty God,
through your Son Jesus Christ you send the Holy Spirit
to be the life and light of all your people:
Open the hearts of these your servants
to the riches of his grace,
that they may bring forth the fruit of the Spirit
in love and joy and peace;
through Jesus Christ our Lord. **Amen.**

Proclaiming and Receiving the Word

One or more readings from the Holy Scriptures.

*Genesis 1: 26-28; Song of Solomon 2: 10-13; 8: 6, 7; Ecclesiastes 3: 1-8;
Ecclesiastes 4: 9-12; Jeremiah 31: 31-34*

Psalm 67, 121, 127, 128

*Romans 12: 5-7,13; 1 Corinthians 13; Ephesians 3: 14-21; Ephesians 4: 1-6;
Ephesians 5: 21-33; Philippians 4: 4-9; Colossians 3: 12-17; 1 John 3: 18-24;
1 John 4: 7-12*

*Matthew 5: 1-10; Matthew 7: 21, 24-27; Mark 10: 6-9,13-16; John 2: 1-11;
John 15: 1-8 or 15: 9-17*

The Marriage

The minister says to the congregation
I am required by law to ask anyone present who knows a reason why ....
and .... may not lawfully marry to declare it now.

The minister says to the couple
The vows you are about to take
are to be made in the name of God,
who is judge of all
and knows all the secrets of our hearts;
therefore if either of you knows any reason
why you may not lawfully marry
you must declare it now.

THE CONSENT

The minister says to the bridegroom
..... will you take .... to be your wife?
Will you love her, comfort her,
honour and care for her,
and, forsaking all others,
be faithful to her as long as you both shall live?

He answers
I will.

The minister says to the bride
.... will you take .... to be your husband?
Will you love him, comfort him,
honour and care for him,
and, forsaking all others,
be faithful to him as long as you both shall live?

She answers
I will.

The bride and bridegroom face each other. The bridegroom takes the bride's right hand in his and says

I .... take you .... to be my wife,

to have and to hold

from this day forward,

for better, for worse,

for richer, for poorer,

in sickness, and in health,

to love and to cherish

till death us do part,

according to God's holy law.

This is my solemn vow.

They loose hands. The bride takes the bridegroom's right hand in hers and says

I .... take you .... to be my husband,

to have and to hold

from this day forward,

for better, for worse,

for richer, for poorer,

in sickness and in health,

to love and to cherish

till death us do part,

according to God's holy law.

This is my solemn vow.

They loose hands.

GIVING AND RECEIVING OF A RING

The minister receives the ring(s) and may say

Heavenly Father,

may *this ring* be to .... and ....

a symbol of unending love and faithfulness

to remind them of the vow and covenant

which they have made this day.

The bridegroom takes the ring and places it on the fourth finger of the bride's
left hand, and holding it there says
I give you this ring
as a sign of our marriage.
With my body I honour you,
and all that I have I share with you
in the name of God,
Father, Son and Holy Spirit.

If this is the one ring used, before they loose hands the bride says
I receive this ring
as a sign of our marriage.
With my body I honour you,
and all that I have I share with you
in the name of God,
Father, Son and Holy Spirit.

If the bride gives a ring, they loose hands and she places it on the fourth finger
of the bridegroom's left hand, and holding it there says
I give you this ring
as a sign of our marriage.
With my body I honour you,
and all that I have I share with you
in the name of God,
Father, Son and Holy Spirit.

THE DECLARATION

The priest addresses the people
In the presence of God, and before this congregation
.... and .... have given their consent
and made their marriage vows to each other.
They have declared their marriage
by the joining of hands
and by the giving and receiving of a ring.
Therefore in the name of God
I pronounce that they are husband and wife.

The priest joins the right hands of the husband and wife together, and says
What God has joined together
let no one put asunder. *Mark 10: 9*

The congregation remains standing.
The husband and wife kneel, and the priest says
God the Father, God the Son, and God the Holy Spirit
bless, preserve and keep you:
the Lord mercifully grant you the riches of his grace
that you may live together in faith and love,
and receive the blessings of eternal life. **Amen.**

The newly married couple may say
O God our Father,
we thank you for uniting our lives
and for giving us to each other in the fulfilment of love.
Watch over us at all times,
guide and protect us,
and give us faith and patience,
that, as we hold each other's hand in yours,
we may draw strength from you
and from each other;
through Jesus Christ our Lord. Amen.

AFFIRMATION BY THE PEOPLE

The priest says
Will you the family and friends of .... and .... support and encourage them
in their marriage?
We will.

THE ACCLAMATIONS

Blessed are you, heavenly Father:
you give joy to the bridegroom and the bride.

Blessed are you, Lord Jesus Christ:
you have brought new life to all your people.

Blessed are you, Holy Spirit of God:
>   **you bring us together in love.**

Blessed be the Father, the Son, and the Holy Spirit:
>   **one God, to be praised for ever. Amen.**

The registration of the marriage may take place now in the church, or at the end of the service.

A psalm or hymn may be sung.

The Prayers

The couple kneel at the Lord's Table.

The prayers are led by the minister or by others appointed by the minister, using either of the following forms. Other prayers may be included.

Silence may be kept.

THE FIRST FORM

Now that .... and .... have given themselves to each other in marriage, let us pray that God will keep them and all other married couples faithful to their marriage vows.

May they live and grow together in love and peace all the days of their life,
>   Lord, in your mercy
>   **hear our prayer.**

May they truly and faithfully perform those vows which they have made together in your sight,
>   Lord, in your mercy
>   **hear our prayer.**

May their life together be a witness to your love in this troubled world; may unity overcome division, forgiveness heal injury, and joy triumph over sorrow,
>   Lord, in your mercy
>   **hear our prayer.**

May their home be a place of love, security and truth, (and may they be blessed with the gift of children),

>Lord, in your mercy
>**hear our prayer.**

We pray for their families and friends, and all who share with them in the happiness of this day,

>Lord, in your mercy
>**hear our prayer.**

We pray for your Church, united to Christ as a bride is to her husband, that it may be faithful to him in love and truthfulness,

>Lord, in your mercy
>**hear our prayer.**

We remember with thankfulness our relatives and friends departed this life in your faith and fear, especially ... and we pray that we may share with them the joys of your eternal kingdom,

>Lord, in your mercy
>**hear our prayer.**

Merciful Father,
accept these our thanksgivings and prayers
for the sake of your Son
our Saviour Jesus Christ. Amen.

Continue on page 27

THE SECOND FORM

One or more of these prayers is said.

For husband and wife
Lord God, faithful from generation to generation,
bless these your servants.
May your word be a lamp to their feet
and a light to their path;
that they may obey your will,
live in safety under your protection,
and abide in your love unto their lives' end;
through Jesus Christ our Lord. **Amen.**

Almighty God, giver of life and love:
Bless .... and .... whom you have now joined in marriage.
Grant them wisdom and devotion in their life together,
that each may be to the other a strength in need,
a comfort in sorrow, and a companion in joy.
So unite their wills in your will
and their spirits in your Spirit,
that they may live and grow together in love and peace
all the days of their life;
through Jesus Christ our Lord. **Amen.**

Almighty and merciful Father,
the strength of all who put their trust in you:
We pray that as you have brought .... and .... together,
you will so enrich them by your grace
that they may truly and faithfully keep those vows
which they have made to one another in your sight;
through Jesus Christ our Lord. **Amen.**

O God, you consecrated marriage
to be a sign of the spiritual unity between Christ and his Church:
Bless these your servants,
that they may love, honour and cherish each other
in faithfulness and patience,
in wisdom and true godliness;
that their home may be a place of blessing and peace;
through Jesus Christ our Lord,
who lives and reigns with you and the Holy Spirit,
one God, now and for ever. **Amen.**

God of all grace, friend and companion,
look in favour on .... and ....
and on all who are made one in marriage.
In your love deepen their love,
strengthen their wills
to keep the promises they have made this day,
that they may continue in life-long faithfulness to each other;
through Jesus Christ our Lord. **Amen.**

God our Creator,
we thank you for your gift of sexual love
by which husband and wife may delight in each other,
and share with you the joy of creating new life.
By your grace may the love of .... and .... remain strong
and may they rejoice in your goodness all their days;
through Jesus Christ our Lord. **Amen.**

For the gift of children
Heavenly Father, maker of all things,
you enable us to share in your work of creation:
Bless this couple with the gift of children,
and give them grace to make their home
a place of love, security and truth,
that their children may grow up to know and love you
in your Son Jesus Christ our Lord. **Amen.**

For Christian witness in marriage
Eternal God, true and loving Father,
in marriage you make your servants one.
May their life together witness to your love
in this troubled world,
may unity overcome division,
forgiveness heal injury,
and joy triumph over sorrow;
through Jesus Christ our Lord. **Amen.**

Almighty God, our heavenly Father,
you gave marriage to be a source of blessing:
We thank you for the joys of family life:
May we know your presence and peace in our homes,
fill them with your love,
and use them for your glory;
through Jesus Christ our Lord. **Amen.**

The couple may say

God of tenderness and strength,
you have brought our paths together
and led us to this day;
go with us now as we travel through good times,
through trouble or through change.
Bless our home, our partings and our meetings.
Make us worthy of each other's best,
and tender with each other's dreams,
trusting in your love in Jesus Christ. Amen.

THE PEACE

The minister says

Jesus said, A new commandment I give to you,
that you love one another:
even as I have loved you, that you also love one another. *John 13: 34*

The peace of the Lord be always with you
and also with you.

It is appropriate that the congregation share with one another a sign of peace.
This may be introduced by the words:

Let us offer one another a sign of peace.

A hymn may be sung.

The bride and bridegroom should receive Holy Communion at the time of their
marriage or at the first opportunity after their marriage.

When Holy Communion is celebrated at the time of the marriage the Holy
Communion begins at Celebrating at the Lord's Table on (BCP page 208) or
in Holy Communion One at **Lift up your hearts** ... *(BCP page 186).*

PROPER PREFACE

We give you thanks
because you have made the union
between Christ and his Church
a pattern for the marriage
between husband and wife:

The minister says

As our Saviour Christ has taught us, so we pray
Our Father in heaven ...

or

As our Saviour Christ has taught us, we are bold to say
Our Father, who art in heaven ...

The minister may say

The grace of our Lord Jesus Christ,
and the love of God,
and the fellowship of the Holy Spirit,
be with us all evermore. **Amen.**

or

God the Holy Trinity
make you strong in faith and love,
defend you on every side,
and guide you in truth and peace:
And the blessing of God Almighty,
the Father, the Son, and the Holy Spirit
be with you, and remain with you always. **Amen.**

NOTES

1 As much notice as possible should be given to the minister of the parish to allow sufficient time for adequate pastoral preparation before marriage.

2 All readings in Proclaiming and Receiving the Word must be from Holy Scripture. These may be used where printed in the service or after The Affirmation by the People. At Holy Communion there are at least two readings, of which the Gospel must be one.

3 Hymns or canticles may be sung at suitable points during the service.

4 The minister and the couple should together choose the readings, hymns, music and the prayers to be used in the service. If a Bible or New Testament is to be presented to the bride and bridegroom it is appropriate that this should be done before the readings.

5 If Holy Communion is celebrated at the marriage, its reception should not be restricted to the bridal party.

On the day of the marriage if anyone alleges or declares any impediment why the man and woman may not lawfully marry, the person alleging or declaring the impediment is required to deposit, or by sureties guarantee, such sum as would cover the cost of the wedding and of all other expenses incurred in connection therewith. The wedding must then be deferred until such time as the truth is tried. Should the impediment not be upheld the amount deposited or guaranteed shall become the property of the man and woman, and the person alleging or declaring the impediment shall be liable for the legal costs incurred.

A FORM OF PRAYER AND DEDICATION
AFTER A CIVIL MARRIAGE

The married couple enter the church together.

The presiding minister says
Grace, mercy and peace
from God our Father and the Lord Jesus Christ
be with you all.
And also with you.

God is love and those who live in love live in God, and God lives in them.
1 John 4: 6

Unless the Lord builds the house, those who labour build in vain.
Psalm 127: 1

.... and .... you stand in the presence of God as husband and wife to dedicate to him your life together, that he may consecrate your marriage and empower you to keep the covenant and promise you have solemnly declared.

The scriptures set before us marriage as part of God's creation
and a holy mystery
in which man and woman become one flesh.
It is God's purpose that, as husband and wife
give themselves to each other
in love throughout their lives,
they shall be united in that love
as Christ is united with his Church.

[Marriage was ordained that husband and wife
may comfort and help each other,
living faithfully together in plenty and in need,

in sorrow and in joy.
It is intended that with delight and tenderness
they may know each other in love,
and through the joy of their bodily union
they may strengthen the union of their hearts and lives.

It is intended that they may be blessed
in the children they may have,
in caring for them and in bringing them up
in accordance with God's will
to his praise and glory.

In marriage husband and wife begin a new life together in the community.
It is a permanent commitment that all should honour.
It must not be undertaken carelessly, lightly or selfishly,
but by God's help, with reverence, responsibility,
respect and the promise to be faithful.]

You now wish to affirm your desire to live together as followers of Christ, and you have come to him, the fountain of grace, that strengthened by the prayers of the Church, you may be enabled to fulfil your marriage vows in love and faithfulness.

A hymn may be sung.

THE COLLECT

The minister says
God our Father,
you have taught us through your Son
that love is the fulfilling of the law.
Grant to your servants that, loving one another,
they may continue in your love until their lives' end:
through Jesus Christ our Lord. **Amen.**

Proclaiming and Receiving the Word

One or more readings from the Scriptures. When there is Holy Communion there are at least two readings, of which the final one is the Gospel.

THE SERMON

A hymn may be sung.

The Dedication

The husband and wife face the minister, who says
.... and .... you have committed yourselves to each other in marriage,
and your marriage is recognised by law.
The Church of Christ understands marriage to be,
in the will of God,
the union of a man and a woman,
for better, for worse,
for richer, for poorer,
in sickness and in health,
to love and to cherish,
till parted by death.
Is this your understanding of the covenant and vow
that you have made?

Husband and wife
It is.

The minister says to the husband
.... you have taken .... to be your wife. Will you continue to love her, comfort her, honour and protect her, and forsaking all others, be faithful to her as long as you both shall live?

He answers
I will.

The minister says to the wife
.... you have taken .... to be your husband. Will you continue to love him, comfort him, honour and protect him, and forsaking all others, be faithful to him as long as you both shall live?

She answers
I will.

The minister may say as the husband and wife join their wedding-ring hands
Heavenly Father, may *these rings* be to .... and .... a symbol of unending love and faithfulness, to remind them of the vow and covenant they have made; through Jesus Christ our Lord. Amen.

The minister says to the congregation
Will you the family and friends of .... and ...., who have gathered here today, continue to support them in their marriage?

The congregation answers
We will.

The husband and wife kneel and say together
Heavenly Father,
we offer you our souls and bodies,
our thoughts and words and deeds,
our love for one another.
Unite our wills in your will,
that we may grow together
in love and peace
all the days of our life;
through Jesus Christ our Lord. Amen.

The minister may say one or both of the following:
Almighty God give you grace to persevere,
that he may complete in you
the work he has already begun;
through Jesus Christ our Lord. **Amen.**

The Lord bless you and watch over you,
the Lord make his face shine upon you
and be gracious to you,
the Lord look kindly on you and give you peace
all the days of your life. **Amen.**

A hymn may be sung.

The couple kneel at the Lord's Table.
The prayers are led by the minister or by others appointed by the minister
using the following or other suitable prayers.

For husband and wife
Lord God,
bless these your servants.
May your word be a lamp to their feet
and a light to their path;
that they may obey your will,
live in safety under your protection,
and abide in your love unto their lives' end;
through Jesus Christ our Lord. **Amen.**

Almighty God, giver of life and love,
bless .... and ...., and all others whom you have joined in marriage.
Grant them wisdom and devotion in their life together,
that each may be to the other
a strength in need, a comfort in sorrow, and a companion in joy.
So unite their wills in your will,
and their spirits in your Spirit,
that they may live and grow together in love and peace
all the days of their life;
through Jesus Christ our Lord. **Amen.**

O God, you consecrated marriage
to be a sign of the spiritual unity
between Christ and his Church:

Bless these your servants,
that they may love, honour and cherish each other
in faithfulness and patience,
in wisdom and true godliness;
that their home may be a place of blessing and peace;
through Jesus Christ our Lord,
who lives and reigns with you and the Holy Spirit,
one God, now and for ever. **Amen.**

God our Creator,
we thank you for your gift of sexual love
by which husband and wife may delight in each other,
and share with you the joy of creating new life.
By your grace may the love of .... and .... remain strong
and may they rejoice in your goodness all their days,
through Jesus Christ our Lord. **Amen.**

For the gift of children
Heavenly Father, maker of all things,
you enable us to share in your work of creation:
Bless this couple with the gift of children,
and give them grace to make their home
a place of love, security and truth,
that their children may grow up to know and love you
in your Son Jesus Christ our Lord. **Amen.**

For Christian witness in marriage
Eternal God, true and loving Father,
in marriage you make your servants one:
May their life together witness to your love
in this troubled world,
may unity overcome division,
forgiveness heal injury,
and joy triumph over sorrow;
through Jesus Christ our Lord. **Amen.**

Almighty God, our heavenly Father,
you gave marriage to be a source of blessing.
We thank you for the joys of family life.
May we know your presence and peace in our homes:
fill them with your love,
and use them for your glory;
through Jesus Christ our Lord. **Amen.**

THE PEACE

The minister says
Jesus said, A new commandment I give to you,
that you love one another:
even as I have loved you, that you also love one another. *John 13: 34*

The peace of the Lord be always with you
and also with you.

It is appropriate that the congregation share with one another a sign of peace.
This may be introduced by the words:
Let us offer one another a sign of peace.

A hymn may be sung.

When Holy Communion Two is celebrated the service continues at Celebrating
at the Lord's Table on (BCP page 208), Holy Communion One at Lift up
your hearts ... *(BCP page 186).*

PROPER PREFACE

We give you thanks
because you have made the union between Christ and his Church
a pattern for the marriage between husband and wife:

THE LORD'S PRAYER

If there is no celebration of Holy Communion the minister says
As our Saviour Christ has taught us, so we pray
Our Father in heaven ...

or
As our Saviour Christ has taught us, we are bold to say
Our Father, who art in heaven ...

The minister may say
The grace of our Lord Jesus Christ,
and the love of God,
and the fellowship of the Holy Spirit,
be with us all evermore. **Amen.**
or
God the Holy Trinity
make you strong in faith and love,
defend you on every side,
and guide you in truth and peace;
and the blessing of God Almighty,
the Father, the Son, and the Holy Spirit
be with you, and remain with you always. **Amen.**

NOTES

1 This service is used at the discretion of the minister. It is one in which the couple, already married, wish to dedicate to God their life together. Because it is not a marriage service, no entry may be made in the register of marriages.

2 Because the marriage has already taken place, no ring is to be given or received in the course of the service.

3 All readings in Proclaiming and Receiving the Word must be from Holy Scripture.

4 The minister and the couple should together choose the readings, hymns, music and the prayers to be used in the service.

5 If Holy Communion is celebrated at this service, all communicants should be free to receive.

Readings at the Marriage Service

Genesis 1: 26-2: 8

God said, 'Let us make humankind in our image, according to our like-ness; and let them have dominion over the fish of the sea, and over the birds of the air, and over the cattle, and over all the wild animals of the earth, and over every creeping thing that creeps upon the earth.'

> So God created humankind in his image,
>> in the image of God he created them;
>> male and female he created them.

God blessed them, and God said to them, 'Be fruitful and multiply, and fill the earth and subdue it; and have dominion over the fish of the sea and over the birds of the air and over every living thing that moves upon the earth.'

Song of Solomon 2: 10-13; 8: 6-7

> My belovèd speaks and says to me:
> 'Arise, my love, my fair one,
>> and come away;
> for now the winter is past,
>> the rain is over and gone.
> The flowers appear on the earth;
>> the time of singing has come,
> and the voice of the turtledove
>> is heard in our land.
> The fig tree puts forth its figs,
>> and the vines are in blossom;
>> they give forth fragrance.
> Arise, my love, my fair one,
>> and come away.

8.6   Set me as a seal upon your heart,
>> as a seal upon your arm;
> for love is strong as death,
>> passion fierce as the grave.

Its flashes are flashes of fire,
  a raging flame.
Many waters cannot quench love,
  neither can floods drown it.
If one offered for love
  all the wealth of one's house,
  it would be utterly scorned.

Jeremiah 31: 31-34

The days are surely coming, says the Lord, when I will make a new covenant with the house of Israel and the house of Judah. It will not be like the covenant that I made with their ancestors when I took them by the hand to bring them out of the land of Egypt – a covenant that they broke, though I was their husband, says the Lord. But this is the covenant that I will make with the house of Israel after those days, says the Lord: I will put my law within them, and I will write it on their hearts; and I will be their God, and they shall be my people. No longer shall they teach one another, or say to each other, 'Know the Lord,' for they shall all know me, from the least of them to the greatest, says the Lord; for I will forgive their iniquity, and remember their sin no more.

PSALMS

Psalm 67

1   God be gracious to us and bless us ▪
      and make his face to shine upon us,

2   That your way may be known upon earth, ▪
      your saving power among all nations.

3†   *Let the peoples praise you, O God;* ▪
      let all the peoples praise you.

4   O let the nations rejoice and be glad, ▪
      for you will judge the peoples righteously
        and govern the nations upon earth.

5.   *Let the peoples praise you, O God;* ▪
      let all the peoples praise you.

6   Then shall the earth bring forth her increase, ▪
      and God, our own God, will bless us.

7   God will bless us, ■
and all the ends of the earth shall fear him.

Psalm 121

1   I lift up my eyes to the hills; ■
from where is my help to come?

2.   My help comes from the Lord, ■
the maker of heaven and earth.

3   He will not suffer your foot to stumble; ■
he who watches over you will not sleep.

4.   Behold, he who keeps watch over Israel ■
shall neither slumber nor sleep.

5   The Lord himself watches over you; ■
the Lord is your shade at your right hand,

6.   So that the sun shall not strike you by day, ■
neither the moon by night.

7   The Lord shall keep you from all evil; ■
it is he who shall keep your soul.

8   The Lord shall keep watch over your going out
      and your coming in, ■
from this time forth for evermore.

Psalm 127

1   Unless the Lord builds the house, ■
those who build it labour in vain.

2   Unless the Lord keeps the city, ■
the guard keeps watch in vain.

3.   It is in vain that you hasten to rise up early
      and go so late to rest, eating the bread of toil, ■
for he gives his beloved sleep.

4   Children are a heritage from the Lord ■
and the fruit of the womb is his gift.

5   Like arrows in the hand of a warrior, ■
so are the children of one's youth.

6   Happy are those who have their quiver full of them: ∎
    they shall not be put to shame
     when they dispute with their enemies in the gate.

Psalm 128

1   Blessed are all those who fear the Lord, ∎
    and walk in his ways.

2   You shall eat the fruit of the toil of your hands; ∎
    it shall go well with you, and happy shall you be.

3.   Your wife within your house shall be like a fruitful vine; ∎
    your children round your table, like fresh olive branches.

4   Thus shall the one be blest ∎
    who fears the Lord.

5   The Lord from out of Zion bless you, ∎
    that you may see Jerusalem in prosperity
     all the days of your life.

6   May you see your children's children, ∎
    and may there be peace upon Israel.

NEW TESTAMENT READINGS

Romans 7: 1-2,9-18

Do you not know, brothers and sisters – for I am speaking to those who know the law – that the law is binding on a person only during that person's lifetime? Thus a married woman is bound by the law to her husband as long as he lives; but if her husband dies, she is discharged from the law concerning the husband.

⁹ I was once alive apart from the law, but when the commandment came, sin revived and I died, and the very commandment that promised life proved to be death to me. For sin, seizing an opportunity in the commandment, deceived me and through it killed me. So the law is holy, and the commandment is holy and just and good.

Did what is good, then, bring death to me? By no means! It was sin, working death in me through what is good, in order that sin might be shown to be sin, and through the commandment might become sinful beyond measure.

For we know that the law is spiritual; but I am of the flesh, sold into slavery under sin. I do not understand my own actions. For I do not do what I want, but I do the very thing I hate. Now if I do what I do not want, I agree that the law is good. But in fact it is no longer I that do it, but sin that dwells within me. For I know that nothing good dwells within me, that is, in my flesh. I can will what is right, but I cannot do it.

Romans 8: 31-35,37-39

What are we to say about these things? If God is for us, who is against us? He who did not withhold his own Son, but gave him up for all of us, will he not with him also give us everything else? Who will bring any charge against God's elect? It is God who justifies. Who is to condemn? It is Christ Jesus, who died, yes, who was raised, who is at the right hand of God, who indeed intercedes for us. Who will separate us from the love of Christ? Will hardship, or distress, or persecution, or famine, or nakedness, or peril, or sword?

[37]No, in all these things we are more than conquerors through him who loved us. For I am convinced that neither death, nor life, nor angels, nor rulers, nor things present, nor things to come, nor powers, nor height, nor depth, nor anything else in all creation, will be able to separate us from the love of God in Christ Jesus our Lord.

Romans 12: 1-2,9-13

I appeal to you therefore, brothers and sisters, by the mercies of God, to present your bodies as a living sacrifice, holy and acceptable to God, which is your spiritual worship. Do not be conformed to this world, but be transformed by the renewing of your minds, so that you may discern what is the will of God – what is good and acceptable and perfect.

[9] Let love be genuine; hate what is evil, hold fast to what is good; love one another with mutual affection; outdo one another in showing honour. Do not lag in zeal, be ardent in spirit, serve the Lord. Rejoice in hope, be patient in suffering, persevere in prayer. Contribute to the needs of the saints; extend hospitality to strangers.

Romans 15: 1-3,5-7,13

We who are strong ought to put up with the failings of the weak, and not to please ourselves. Each of us must please our neighbour for the good purpose of building up the neighbour. For Christ did not please himself;

but, as it is written, 'The insults of those who insult you have fallen on me.' May the God of steadfastness and encouragement grant you to live in harmony with one another, in accordance with Christ Jesus, so that together you may with one voice glorify the God and Father of our Lord Jesus Christ.

Welcome one another, therefore, just as Christ has welcomed you, for the glory of God.

May the God of hope fill you with all joy and peace in believing, so that you may abound in hope by the power of the Holy Spirit.

1 Corinthians 13

If I speak in the tongues of mortals and of angels, but do not have love, I am a noisy gong or a clanging cymbal. And if I have prophetic powers, and understand all mysteries and all knowledge, and if I have all faith, so as to remove mountains, but do not have love, I am nothing. If I give away all my possessions, and if I hand over my body so that I may boast, but do not have love, I gain nothing.

Love is patient; love is kind; love is not envious or boastful or arrogant or rude. It does not insist on its own way; it is not irritable or resentful; it does not rejoice in wrongdoing, but rejoices in the truth. It bears all things, believes all things, hopes all things, endures all things.

Love never ends. But as for prophecies, they will come to an end; as for tongues, they will cease; as for knowledge, it will come to an end. For we know only in part, and we prophesy only in part; but when the complete comes, the partial will come to an end. When I was a child, I spoke like a child, I thought like a child, I reasoned like a child; when I became an adult, I put an end to childish ways. For now we see in a mirror, dimly, but then we will see face to face. Now I know only in part; then I will know fully, even as I have been fully known. And now faith, hope, and love abide, these three; and the greatest of these is love.

Ephesians 3: 14-21

I bow my knees before the Father, from whom every family in heaven and on earth takes its name. I pray that, according to the riches of his glory, he may grant that you may be strengthened in your inner being with power through his Spirit, and that Christ may dwell in your hearts through faith, as you are being rooted and grounded in love. I pray that you may have the power to comprehend, with all the saints, what is the breadth and length and height and depth, and to know the love of Christ that surpasses knowledge, so that you may be filled with all the fullness of God.

Now to him who by the power at work within us is able to accomplish abundantly far more than all we can ask or imagine, to him be glory in the church and in Christ Jesus to all generations, for ever and ever. Amen.

Ephesians 4: 1-6

I, the prisoner in the Lord, beg you to lead a life worthy of the calling to which you have been called, with all humility and gentleness, with patience, bearing with one another in love, making every effort to maintain the unity of the Spirit in the bond of peace. There is one body and one Spirit, just as you were called to the one hope of your calling, one Lord, one faith, one baptism, one God and Father of all, who is above all and through all and in all.

Ephesians 5: 21-33

Be subject to one another out of reverence for Christ.

Wives, be subject to your husbands as you are to the Lord. For the husband is the head of the wife just as Christ is the head of the church, the body of which he is the Saviour. Just as the church is subject to Christ, so also wives ought to be, in everything, to their husbands.

Husbands, love your wives, just as Christ loved the church and gave himself up for her, in order to make her holy by cleansing her with the washing of water by the word, so as to present the church to himself in splendour, without a spot or wrinkle or anything of the kind – yes, so that she may be holy and without blemish. In the same way, husbands should love their wives as they do their own bodies. He who loves his wife loves himself. For no one ever hates his own body, but he nourishes and tenderly cares for it, just as Christ does for the church, because we are members of his body. 'For this reason a man will leave his father and mother and be joined to his wife, and the two will become one flesh.' This is a great mystery, and I am applying it to Christ and the church. Each of you, however, should love his wife as himself, and a wife should respect her husband.

Philippians 4: 4-9

Rejoice in the Lord always; again I will say, Rejoice. Let your gentleness be known to everyone. The Lord is near. Do not worry about anything, but in everything by prayer and supplication with thanksgiving let your requests be made known to God. And the peace of God, which surpasses all understanding, will guard your hearts and your minds in Christ Jesus. Finally, belovèd, whatever is true, whatever is honourable, whatever is just, whatever is pure, whatever is pleasing, whatever is commendable, if there is any excellence and if there is anything worthy of praise, think about these things. Keep on doing the things that you have learned and received and heard and seen in me, and the God of peace will be with you.

Colossians 3: 12-17

As God's chosen ones, holy and belovèd, clothe yourselves with compassion, kindness, humility, meekness, and patience. Bear with one another and, if anyone has a complaint against another, forgive each other; just as the Lord has forgiven you, so you also must forgive. Above all, clothe yourselves with love, which binds everything together in perfect harmony. And let the peace of Christ rule in your hearts, to which indeed you were called in the one body. And be thankful. Let the word of Christ dwell in you richly; teach and admonish one another in all wisdom; and with gratitude in your hearts sing psalms, hymns, and spiritual songs to God. And whatever you do, in word or deed, do everything in the name of the Lord Jesus, giving thanks to God the Father through him.

1 John 3: 18-24

Little children, let us love, not in word or speech, but in truth and action. And by this we will know that we are from the truth and will reassure our hearts before him whenever our hearts condemn us; for God is greater than our hearts, and he knows everything. Belovèd, if our hearts do not condemn us, we have boldness before God; and we receive from him whatever we ask, because we obey his commandments and do what pleases him.

And this is his commandment, that we should believe in the name of his Son Jesus Christ and love one another, just as he has commanded us. All who obey his commandments abide in him, and he abides in them. And by this we know that he abides in us, by the Spirit that he has given us.

1 John 4: 7-12

Belovèd, let us love one another, because love is from God; everyone who loves is born of God and knows God. Whoever does not love does not know God, for God is love. God's love was revealed among us in this way: God sent his only Son into the world so that we might live through him. In this is love, not that we loved God but that he loved us and sent his Son to be the atoning sacrifice for our sins. Belovèd, since God loved us so much, we also ought to love one another. No one has ever seen God; if we love one another, God lives in us, and his love is perfected in us.

GOSPEL READINGS

Matthew 5: 1-10

When Jesus saw the crowds, he went up the mountain; and after he sat down, his disciples came to him. Then he began to speak, and taught them, saying:

'Blessèd are the poor in spirit, for theirs is the kingdom of heaven.

'Blessèd are those who mourn, for they will be comforted.

'Blessèd are the meek, for they will inherit the earth.

'Blessèd are those who hunger and thirst for righteousness,
    for they will be filled.

'Blessèd are the merciful, for they will receive mercy.

'Blessèd are the pure in heart, for they will see God.

'Blessèd are the peacemakers, for they will be called
    children of God.

'Blessèd are those who are persecuted for righteousness' sake,
    for theirs is the kingdom of heaven.'

Matthew 7: 21,24-29

Jesus said, 'Not everyone who says to me, "Lord, Lord," will enter the kingdom of heaven, but only the one who does the will of my Father in heaven. [24]'Everyone then who hears these words of mine and acts on them will be like a wise man who built his house on rock. The rain fell, the floods came, and the winds blew and beat on that house, but it did not fall, because it had been founded on rock. And everyone who hears these words of mine and does not act on them will be like a foolish man who built his house on sand. The rain fell, and the floods came, and the winds blew and beat against that house, and it fell – and great was its fall!'

Now when Jesus had finished saying these things, the crowds were astounded at his teaching, for he taught them as one having authority, and not as their scribes.

Mark 10: 6-9,13-16

Jesus said to the Pharisees, 'From the beginning of creation, "God made them male and female." "For this reason a man shall leave his father and mother and be joined to his wife, and the two shall become one flesh." So they are no longer two, but one flesh. Therefore what God has joined together, let no one separate.'

¹³People were bringing little children to him in order that he might touch them; and the disciples spoke sternly to them. But when Jesus saw this, he was indignant and said to them, 'Let the little children come to me; do not stop them; for it is to such as these that the kingdom of God belongs. Truly I tell you, whoever does not receive the kingdom of God as a little child will never enter it.' And he took them up in his arms, laid his hands on them, and blessed them.

John 2: 1-11

On the third day there was a wedding in Cana of Galilee, and the mother of Jesus was there. Jesus and his disciples had also been invited to the wedding. When the wine gave out, the mother of Jesus said to him, 'They have no wine.' And Jesus said to her, 'Woman, what concern is that to you and to me? My hour has not yet come.' His mother said to the servants, 'Do whatever he tells you.' Now standing there were six stone water jars for the Jewish rites of purification, each holding twenty or thirty gallons. Jesus said to them, 'Fill the jars with water.' And they filled them up to the brim. He said to them, 'Now draw some out, and take it to the chief steward.' So they took it. When the steward tasted the water that had become wine, and did not know where it came from (though the servants who had drawn the water knew), the steward called the bridegroom and said to him, 'Everyone serves the good wine first, and then the inferior wine after the guests have become drunk. But you have kept the good wine until now.' Jesus did this, the first of his signs, in Cana of Galilee, and revealed his glory; and his disciples believed in him.

John 15: 1-8

John 15: 1-8

Jesus said to his disciples, 'I am the true vine, and my Father is the vine-grower. He removes every branch in me that bears no fruit. Every branch that bears fruit he prunes to make it bear more fruit. You have already been cleansed by the word that I have spoken to you. Abide in me as I abide in you. Just as the branch cannot bear fruit by itself unless it abides in the vine, neither can you unless you abide in me. I am the vine, you are the branches. Those who abide in me and I in them bear much fruit, because apart from me you can do nothing. Whoever does not abide in me is thrown away like a branch and withers; such branches are gathered, thrown into the fire, and burned. If you abide in me, and my words abide in you, ask for whatever you wish, and it will be done for you. My Father is glorified by this, that you bear much fruit and become my disciples.'

John 15: 9-17

Jesus said to his disciples, 'As the Father has loved me, so I have loved you; abide in my love. If you keep my commandments, you will abide in my love, just as I have kept my Father's commandments and abide in his love. I have said these things to you so that my joy may be in you, and that your joy may be complete.

'This is my commandment, that you love one another as I have loved you. No one has greater love than this, to lay down one's life for one's friends. You are my friends if you do what I command you. I do not call you servants any longer, because the servant does not know what the master is doing; but I have called you friends, because I have made known to you everything that I have heard from my Father. You did not choose me but I chose you. And I appointed you to go and bear fruit, fruit that will last, so that the Father will give you whatever you ask him in my name. I am giving you these commands so that you may love one another.'